Vegetables

BY ALLISON LASSIEUR

Smart Apple Media

P.O. Box 3263, Mankato, MN 56002
www.blackrabbitbooks.com

Cataloging-in-Publication Data is available from the Library of Congress
ISBN: 978-162588-288-2

Published by arrangement with Amicus.

Editors: Rebecca Glaser and Tram Bui
Series Designer: Kathleen Petelinsek
Book Designer: Heather Dreisbach
Photo Researcher: Kurtis Kinneman

Photo Credits: Lauri Patterson/Getty Images, cover; alexmak72427/Shutterstock, 5; vallefrias/Shutterstock, 6; Dan Kosmayer/Shutterstock, 9; Andris Tkacenko/Shutterstock, 10; Ivonne Wierink/Shutterstock, 12–13; Kingarion/Shutterstock, 14; H. Mark Weidman Photography/Alamy, 17; Dennis MacDonald/Alamy, 18; Lily8/Shutterstock, 21; MBI/Alamy, 22; Rob Walls/Alamy, 25; Tips Images/SuperStock, 26; Vezzani Photography/Shutterstock, 29

Printed in the United States of America at Corporate Graphics in North Mankato, Minnesota.

10 9 8 7 6 5 4 3 2 1

Table of Contents

What Are Vegetables?

What is a vegetable? A **vegetable** is a part of a plant that you can eat. Some vegetables are leaves, such as spinach and lettuce. A potato is a root. So are carrots. Celery comes from a plant's stem. Broccoli is actually a flower bud!

Carrots and leeks are
roots of the plant.

Cucumbers are actually fruits.

Q What vegetables are really fruits?

What is the difference between vegetables and fruits? There are two big things! The first is that vegetables come from many different parts of a plant. A fruit is only the part of a plant that covers the seeds. The second is how they taste. Veggies are **savory**. Fruits are sweet.

A Tomatoes, pumpkins, olives, and cucumbers. They cover the seeds of the plant.

Has anyone told you to eat your vegetables? Moms and dads love to say this. They are not being mean. Vegetables have more vitamins and **nutrients** than almost any other food. And check out their bright colors. The more colorful they are, the better they are for you. So eat a veggie rainbow!

Q Should you eat vegetables *every* day?

Vegetables can be many colors.

A

Yes! Kids should eat 1½ cups (375 mL) of veggies every day. A salad, a potato, a large ear of corn, or 12 baby carrots count as 1 cup (250 mL).

Weeding the garden helps the veggies grow.

Q What are the most well-liked vegetables in the U.S.?

Where Do Vegetables Grow?

Vegetables are not hard to grow. All they need are sun, food, and water. They grow best with at least six hours of sun a day.

Some crops grow better in certain places. A cool **climate** keeps mold from growing on potatoes in Idaho. Sweet onions grow well in Georgia where it's warm.

A Tomatoes are number one! Second are potatoes. Lettuce is third.

What does a garden look like? You may think of a big patch of dirt outside. The vegetables grow in straight rows. But vegetables can grow anywhere! You don't have to have a big yard. Plants can grow in pots and baskets. Some people plant vegetables in wooden boxes.

Vegetables can grow in small boxes.

A greenhouse keeps the air warm. Plants can grow even when it is cold outside.

Q What countries grow vegetables that we eat in winter?

Traveling Vegetables

Most vegetables grow in summer. So how can you buy them fresh in the winter? Vegetables grow around the world. Mexico has a warm climate. Crops grow there when it is winter in the United States. Farmers in Canada grow crops in **greenhouses** when it gets too cold to grow outside. They ship the food to stores in the U.S.

A Mexico grows cucumbers, peppers, and tomatoes. Asparagus comes fresh from Peru.

Vegetables don't always have to travel far. Farmers near your town grow lots of vegetables. At a **farmers' market**, you can meet the farmers who grow your food. You can ask them questions. Buying food locally helps farmers who live near you. You get freshly picked food, too!

At a farmers' market, you can meet local farmers who grow veggies.

Did you know that some vegetables grow better in spring or fall? Farmers decide what to grow based on where they live and the time of year. Carrots grow from July to December. You can eat fresh sweet corn from July until October. Do you like fresh lettuce? It grows from April until November.

Fresh corn grows better in summer.

Vegetables Around the World

Some vegetables travel far to get to your plate. Have you ever eaten kohlrabi? It is popular in Germany. It looks like a turnip, but it tastes like sweet broccoli! How about a nopal cactus? It comes from Mexico. It tastes like a mix of watermelon and bubble gum. It is good in salsa.

People in Germany eat kohlrabi.

Chickpeas can go in many foods.

Q What is another name for chickpeas?

Chickpeas come from Asia. Have you tried them? If so, you've had a food that people have eaten for thousands of years! They are popular in soups, stews, and salads. You can mash chickpeas and mix them with spices to make hummus. Hummus is a yummy dip for bread or veggies.

A Garbanzo beans.

People around the world eat all sorts of veggies that may seem strange to you. People in Iceland eat dulse, a type of seaweed. It can be served fresh or dried with fish. People in Japan also eat seaweed. They use it to make sushi. In Italy, people eat a spiky cauliflower called romanesco. It looks like it has lime green pine trees all over it. It has a crunchy, nutty flavor.

Romanesco is eaten in Italy.

Cooked veggies are a healthy meal.

Healthy Vegetables

Vegetables are good for you. That's a no-brainer. But do you know why they're so great? Veggies are filled with vitamins, nutrients, and fiber. They can help protect against some kinds of cancers. They keep you from getting heart disease. There is no downside to eating veggies. They are like the superheroes of food!

How many vegetables should you eat? Half your plate should be filled with fruits and vegetables. It's easy to eat veggies every day. Make a ranch dip for carrots. Snack on crunchy veggies and salsa. Eat a small salad with lunch and dinner. Trying out new ways to eat food will make eating veggies fun!

Q Okay, you hate veggies. Is there any way to make them taste better?

Veggies can be dipped in ranch for a great snack!

A Yes! Hide them in other foods. Blend a bunch of vegetables. Then mix them into brownies or pizza sauce. You won't even taste the veggies.

Glossary

climate The usual weather in a place.

farmers' market A place where farmers sell their vegetables.

greenhouse A building where people protect and grow plants and vegetables during any season.

nutrient Something that is needed by people to stay strong and healthy.

savory Having a pleasing taste that is not sweet.

vegetable An edible part of a plant that is not sweet.

Read More

Cleary, Brian P. *Green Beans, Potatoes, and Even Tomatoes: What is in the Vegetables Group?* Minneapolis: Millbrook Press, 2011.

Cornell, Kari. *Terrific Veggies on the Side.* Minneapolis: Millbrook Press, 2014.

Owen, Ruth. *Vegetables! Life on a Produce Farm.* New York: Windmill Books, 2012.

Schuh, Mari. *Vegetables on MyPlate.* Mankato, Minn.: Capstone Press, 2013.

Websites

Eating Well with Canada's Food Guide
www.hc-sc.gc.ca/fn-an/food-guide-aliment/index-eng.php

Fruit and Veggie Color Champions
www.foodchamps.org/

MyPlate Kids' Place
www.choosemyplate.gov/kids/index.html

Every effort has been made to ensure that these websites are appropriate for children. However, because of the nature of the Internet, it is impossible to guarantee that these sites will remain active indefinitely or that their contents will not be altered.

Index

About the Author

Allison Lassieur tries to eat plenty of fresh, good foods at every meal. She has written more than 100 books for kids. Allison especially likes to write about history, food, and science. She lives in a house in the woods with her husband, daughter, three dogs, two cats, and a blue fish named Marmalade.